THOMAS JEFFERSON

A Photo-Illustrated Biography
by T.M. Usel

Historical Consultant
Steve Potts
Professor of History

Bridgestone Books
an Imprint of Capstone Press

Facts about Thomas Jefferson

- Thomas Jefferson took 17 days to write the Declaration of Independence.
- Only one of his children lived longer than he did.
- He did not like the Constitution until it had a Bill of Rights.
- He bought the Louisiana Territory from France for $15 million.

Bridgestone Books are published by Capstone Press • 818 North Willow Street, Mankato, Minnesota 56001
Copyright © 1996 by Capstone Press • All rights reserved • Printed in the United States of America

Library of Congress Cataloging-in-Publication Data
Usel, T.M.
    Thomas Jefferson, a photo-illustrated biography/T.M. Usel.
    p. cm.
    Includes bibliographical references and index.
    Summary: Presents the life story of the third president of the United States, who authored the Declaration of Independence and is known for his ability as an inventor and architect.
    ISBN 1-56065-343-4
    1. Jefferson, Thomas, 1743-1826--Juvenile literature. 2. Jefferson, Thomas, 1743-1826--Pictorial works--Juvenile literature. 3. Presidents--United States--Biography--Juvenile literature. 4. Presidents--United States--Pictorial works--Juvenile literature. [1.Jefferson, Thomas, 1743-1826. 2. Presidents.] I. Title.
E332.79.U82 1996
973.4'6'092--dc20
[B]

        95-46664
        CIP
        AC

Photo credits
Archive Photos: 16, 18
Bettmann Archive: cover, 4, 6, 10, 12, 14
Corbis-Bettmann: 8, 20

Table of Contents

Words in **boldface** type in the text are defined in the Words to Know section in the back of this book.

Man of Many Talents

Thomas Jefferson was the third president of the United States.

He is best remembered for writing the Declaration of Independence. In this document, the 13 American colonies declared their independence from England. It was adopted on July 4, 1776. It marked the birth of the United States as a nation.

But Thomas Jefferson did much more than give Americans a reason to celebrate the Fourth of July. He was an inventor, a writer, and a musician. He was a farmer, an architect, and a book lover. He was a man of many talents.

Thomas Jefferson lived at a time when tradition and governments were being questioned. He helped the United States become independent. He fought to make it a better country. Thomas Jefferson made it a bigger country, too. The United States doubled in size while he was president.

Thomas Jefferson wrote the Declaration of Independence.

Early Life

Thomas Jefferson was born on April 2, 1743, in the **colony** of Virginia. He was the first child born to Peter and Jane Jefferson. He had six sisters and one brother.

Nine years after Thomas was born, the calendar changed. This moved Thomas's birthday to April 13.

The Jeffersons lived on a farm called Shadwell. When Thomas was two, his family moved to Tuckahoe, the farm of William Randolph, who had died. Thomas's father had promised to take care of the Randolph children when their father died.

When Thomas was nine, his family moved back to Shadwell. Thomas went to **boarding school** instead of moving with the family. He still spent his summers at Shadwell, though.

His father died when Thomas was 14. Thomas moved home to Shadwell to care for his family.

Thomas was the first child born to Peter and Jane Jefferson.

Thomas's Family

Thomas went to the College of William and Mary in Williamsburg, Virginia. He became a lawyer, and in 1767, he opened up a law office there.

But Thomas wanted to return to Shadwell. He wanted to build a beautiful house on a hill there. He would call it Monticello. That means "little mountain" in Italian and is pronounced Mont-i-chel-lo.

In 1769, Thomas was elected to the Virginia **House of Burgesses**. That same year, he turned over a set of plans to builders. They were the designs for Monticello. Thomas was ready to start work on his future home.

Thomas married Martha Wayles Skelton on New Year's Day, 1772. In September, their daughter was born. They named her Martha but called her Patsy. She was the first of six children. She was the only one of Thomas's children to outlive him.

Martha, who was called Patsy, was Thomas's only child to outlive him.

Return to Monticello

In 1773, Martha's father died. He left one-third of his estate to Thomas and Martha. They **inherited** 11,000 acres of land and 135 slaves. Added to what they already owned, this made them quite wealthy. Thomas gave up his law practice to stay at Monticello.

Thomas preferred farming at Monticello to politics. Still, he spent much of his time in Williamsburg, then the capital of Virginia. He was working so the colonies could govern themselves. Thomas felt that England treated the colonies poorly.

Thomas and other Virginia leaders came up with a plan. They wanted men from all the colonies to meet at a Continental Congress. There they would decide what to do about the British. At 32, Thomas was one of the youngest **delegates** to the Second Continental Congress. The delegates decided that the colonies should become independent of England.

Jefferson designed and built his home and named it Monticello.

Declaration of Independence

Delegates to the Second Continental Congress met in the spring of 1776. They asked Thomas and a few others to write a declaration of independence.

Thomas spent 17 days writing and rewriting the formal declaration of independence. Others made suggestions. But the document was mostly Thomas's work. It says that all men are created equal. It says everyone has the right to life, liberty, and the pursuit of happiness.

Thomas finished writing the Declaration of Independence on June 28, 1776. The congress debated what it said while Thomas sat silently. On July 4, the declaration was adopted.

The first shots in the Revolutionary War had been fired in 1775. The fighting finally ended in 1781. The Americans won the war and their independence from England.

The Declaration of Independence was adopted on July 4, 1776.

A Career in Politics

During the war, in 1779, Thomas was elected governor of Virginia. British soldiers landed in Virginia and almost captured Thomas. But he escaped.

Thomas retired as governor in 1781, the same year the war ended. But he did not retire for long. In 1783, Thomas was elected to Congress.

The following year Congress sent Thomas to France to negotiate trade treaties. When Benjamin Franklin resigned as ambassador to France, Thomas replaced him.

While in Paris, Thomas received a copy of the **Constitution**. He liked parts of it, but he worried that it did not have a bill of rights. He urged that amendments to protect individual rights be added, and they were.

Thomas also received word that Virginia had passed a bill he had written. The bill guaranteed religious freedom in the state.

It was Thomas's idea to add a bill of rights to the Constitution.

The Presidency

Thomas became the third president of the United States in 1801. First he had served as secretary of state for President George Washington. He had also served as vice president for John Adams, who was the country's second president.

As president, Thomas is most remembered for buying the Louisiana Territory from France. The territory contained all of the land between the Mississippi River and the Rocky Mountains. This purchase of land for only $15 million doubled the size of the United States.

Thomas doubted that the Constitution allowed the purchase of the new territory. But he and the Senate felt that the benefits to the country were important. They were willing to risk breaking the law.

Thomas's secretary, Meriwether Lewis, and William Clark explored the new territory and beyond. They reached the Pacific Ocean in 1805.

Thomas Jefferson bought the Louisiana Territory from France.

Home at Last

Thomas won re-election as president but did not seek a third term. He retired from politics and returned to his beloved Monticello.

Thomas stayed busy. He read books and wrote many letters. Through the years he had invented clever devices. He made a revolving music stand and a device to bring his clothes to him from his closet. He invented a device for writing two copies of a letter at the same time. He won a prize for a plow he invented.

Thomas was lonely without his wife, Martha. She had died in 1782 after giving birth to their sixth child. His children were dead, too, except for Patsy. She and her family came to live with Thomas. His slave, Sally Hemings, was there, too.

Some historians believe Thomas had several children with Sally. In his will, he freed five of Sally's sons. Sally was later freed by Patsy.

Thomas's many inventions included a portable writing desk.

Founder of the University of Virginia

Thomas was especially proud of establishing the University of Virginia. Thomas designed the buildings and raised the money to build them. He supervised the construction and hired the staff. The University of Virginia opened on March 7, 1825. It is in Charlottesville, not far from Monticello.

In 1826, Thomas became ill. He died on July 4 at the age of 83. He died on the 50th anniversary of the signing of the Declaration of Independence.

Thomas did much in his lifetime. But he valued three of his accomplishments the most. He wrote the following words for his gravestone:

Here was buried
Thomas Jefferson
Author of the
Declaration of American Independence
of the Statute of Virginia for Religious Freedom
and Father of the University of Virginia.

Thomas Jefferson established the University of Virginia.

Words from Thomas Jefferson

"With respect to the distribution of your time the following is what I should approve.

from 8. to 10 o'clock practice music

from 10. to 1. dance one day and draw another

from 1. to 2. draw on the day you dance, and write a letter the next day

from 3. to 4. read French

from 4. to 5. exercise yourself in music

from 5. till bedtime read English, write etc.

I expect you will write to me by every post. Inform me what books you read, what tunes you learn, and inclose me your best copy of every lesson in drawing."

From a 1783 letter Jefferson wrote to his daughter, Patsy, age 11.

Important Dates in Thomas Jefferson's Life

1743 – Born on April 13 in Albemarle County, Virginia

1768 – Elected to House of Burgesses; construction of Monticello begins

1772 – Marries Martha Wayles Skelton

1776 – Writes the Declaration of Independence

1779 – Elected governor of Virginia

1782 – Martha Jefferson dies

1783 – Elected to Continental Congress

1784 – Becomes minister to France

1796 – Becomes vice president under John Adams

1801 – Takes office as third president of the United States

1803 – Louisiana Purchase

1825 – University of Virginia opens

1826 – Dies on July 4, 50th anniversary of the Declaration of Independence

Words To Know

boarding school—a school where students live

colony—group of people who settle in a distant land but remain under control of their native country. The 13 British colonies in North America became the original United States.

Constitution—the document that is the basic law of the United States

delegate—person chosen to speak and act for others

House of Burgesses—the lower house of the colonial legislature of Virginia

inherit—receive from someone who has died

Read More

Adler, David. *A Picture Book of Thomas Jefferson.* New York: Holiday House, 1990.

Giblin, James Cross. *Thomas Jefferson: A Picture Book Biography.* New York: Scholastic, 1994.

Green, Carol. *Thomas Jefferson: Author, Inventor, President.* Chicago: Children's Press, 1991.

Oakley, Ruth. *The Marshall Cavendish Illustrated History of Presidents of the United States.* New York: Marshall Cavendish, 1990.

Useful Addresses

Monticello
P.O. Box 316
Charlottesville, VA 22902

Jefferson Memorial
900 Ohio Drive SW
Washington, DC 20242

Colonial Williamsburg Foundation
P.O. Box 1776
Williamsburg, VA 23187-1776

Declaration House
313 Walnut Street
Philadelphia, PA 19106

Index